WHO DISCOVERED AMERICA?

Valerie Wyatt

With illustrations by Howie Woo

Kids Can Press

For Valerie Hussey

Acknowledgments

Every book is a group project, and this one involved many people. My thanks to Howie Woo for his charming illustrations. Also thanks to Elizabeth Lane, volunteer, and Kristina Leedberg, Head of Information Services, J.V. Fletcher Library, Westford, MA; Dr. Birgitta Wallace, retired archaeologist, Parks Canada, Atlantic Service Centre, Halifax; Cleone Hawkinson, President, Friends of Americas Past; Dr. Douglas W. Owsley, Curator, Division Head, Physical Anthropology, Smithsonian Institution; Dr. Tom Dillehay, Department of Anthropology, Vanderbilt University. My special thanks to Dr. Ruth Gruhn, Professor Emerita, University of Alberta, for reviewing the prehistory information and answering my many queries with such patience and care. And most of all, thank you to editor Kathy Vanderlinden and designer Julia Naimska for their creativity, talent and friendship.

Text © 2008 Valerie Wyatt
Illustrations © 2008 Kids Can Press

Kids Can Press acknowledges the financial support of the Government of Ontario, through the Ontario Media Development Corporation's Ontario Book Initiative; the Ontario Arts Council; the Canada Council for the Arts; and the Government of Canada, through the BPIDP, for our publishing activity.

Published in Canada by
Kids Can Press Ltd.
29 Birch Avenue
Toronto, ON M4V 1E2

Published in the U.S. by
Kids Can Press Ltd.
2250 Military Road
Tonawanda, NY 14150

www.kidscanpress.com

Edited by Kathy Vanderlinden
Designed by Julia Naimska
Illustrated by Howie Woo
Printed and bound in China

The hardcover edition of this book is smyth sewn casebound.
The paperback edition of this book is limp sewn with a drawn-on cover.

CM 08 0 9 8 7 6 5 4 3 2 1
CM PA 08 0 9 8 7 6 5 4 3 2 1

Library and Archives Canada Cataloguing in Publication

Wyatt, Valerie
    Who discovered America? / Valerie Wyatt.

Includes index.
ISBN 978-1-55453-128-8 (bound). ISBN 978-1-55453-129-5 (pbk.)

1. America—Discovery and exploration—Pre-Columbian—Juvenile literature. 2. America—Antiquities—Juvenile literature. 3. America—Discovery and exploration—Juvenile literature. I. Title.

E101.W94 2008   j970.01'1   C2007-906082-X

Kids Can Press is a *lorus*™ Entertainment company

CONTENTS

WHO DISCOVERED AMERICA?

IMAGINE DISCOVERING A COMPLETELY new land. You would set foot on soil that had never been marked with a human footprint. Your eyes would see sights that no one had seen before. You would be the first!

Now imagine that the land was America. Long before there were towns or cities or farms or even roads, someone was the very first person to discover America. But who was that person?

Was it Christopher Columbus, who sailed to the Americas in 1492? For a long time, people *did* think Columbus was the discoverer. But recently, historians and scientists have been questioning that claim. Like detectives trying to solve a mystery, they have searched in Chinese libraries, under mounds of soil in Newfoundland and on the bottom of the Pacific Ocean — anywhere and everywhere there is evidence of people coming to America. And they have come up with some pretty fascinating and far-out ideas.

So who did discover America? Turn the page to take a journey back in time and meet the main contenders.

Today there are no new lands to discover — at least not here on Earth. But in 1969, U.S. astronaut Neil Armstrong did discover a new land — our moon. He had the thrill of being first to leave his footprint there. Here it is. Because there is no rain or wind on the moon to wear it down, his footprint should last for about a million years.

ACTUALLY, IT'S THE AMERICAS

This book is about all of the Americas — North, South and Central — because clues to the mystery of who got here first are scattered all over the western hemisphere. The Americas are shown in green on this map.

CHRISTOPHER COLUMBUS SAILS THE OCEAN BLUE

CHRISTOPHER COLUMBUS IS SO FAMOUS there is a country (Colombia), a city (Columbus, Ohio) and a river (the Columbia) named after him. There are also Columbus parks, squares, highways and schools — all because he is known as the man who discovered America.

The funny thing is, Columbus never set out in search of a new land. He had been sent by the king and queen of Spain to find a westward route to the Indies (now India and Southeast Asia). Spain was hooked on the spices of the Indies, but the usual eastward route there was blocked by unfriendly Mongols. And so a new way was needed.

FLYAWAY ISLANDS

Stare hard at this picture. Really hard. See that island off in the distance, near the horizon? If so, you've been fooled, just as sailors have been fooled for hundreds of years.

Clouds on the western horizon at sunset often look like islands — until they float off. That's why Columbus's crew kept sounding false alarms. They thought they'd seen land, but they'd just been tricked by a flyaway island.

Columbus (who may have been Italian) sailed west from Palos, Spain, on August 3, 1492. His three ships — the *Niña,* the *Pinta* and the *Santa Maria* — stopped for a month in the Canary Islands to take on supplies and do some repairs before heading into the unknown.

A big reward — 10 000 maravedis, the equivalent of fifteen months' pay for an ordinary seaman — had been offered to the crew member who first spotted land. On September 25, a sailor on watch on the *Pinta* suddenly shouted, *"Tierra!"* (Land!). The ships sailed on, eager to find the land the sailor had seen. But it was a false alarm. Three more false alarms were sounded over the next two-and-a-half weeks, and with each the crew grew more irritable.

Then, at two o'clock on the morning of October 12, another call of *"Tierra! Tierra!"* rang out. Bleary-eyed sailors grumbled themselves awake. *If this is another false alarm …* But this time, it was the real thing. Later that morning, Columbus set foot on … well, no one knows for certain where. The most likely place is the island of Guanahani (Columbus renamed it San Salvador) in the Bahamas. The Americas were officially discovered.

Columbus befriended the aboriginal people, searched for gold, explored some more and, when the *Santa Maria* ran aground, started a settlement for the thirty-nine men he had to leave behind. He sailed back to Europe with gold, tobacco, pineapples, turkey, hammocks and even some kidnapped aboriginal people — all new to Europe. He was given a hero's welcome and was on his way to becoming a legend.

Three more trips to the Americas followed. Columbus explored many of the Caribbean islands and even landed on the mainland of South America. His relations with the aboriginal people soured as he claimed their lands for Spain and took many slaves.

Columbus died in Spain in 1506 believing he had found … the Indies. Yes, the great explorer never knew he was the discoverer of a brand-new land, the Americas.

Or was he?

This is a replica of the **Santa Maria,** *one of Columbus's ships.*

THE REAL THING

IF YOU FIND YOURSELF ON AVENIDA DA Liberdade (Liberty Avenue) in Lisbon, Portugal, look for a mosaic on the pavement in memory of the man who discovered America. It says:

JOÃO VAZ CORTE-REAL DESCOBRIDOR DA AMERICA
(João Vaz Corte-Real Discoverer of America)

That's right — not Columbus, but Corte-Real. Even more surprising is the date that Corte-Real is said to have made this famous discovery: 1472 — twenty years *before* Columbus.

The problem is that proof of Corte-Real's voyage hasn't survived or simply doesn't exist, even though stories about it do. According to these stories, Corte-Real sailed by ship first to Iceland and then on to Newfoundland.

Three scraps of evidence support this idea. One, Corte-Real was rewarded by the king of Portugal for his discovery of *"Terra do Bacalhau"* (Land of the Cod), which might have meant Newfoundland, whose waters were teeming with codfish. Two, a map of Newfoundland published about fifty years after the trip shows two places named after João Vaz Corte-Real. Three, a letter sent to the Danish king about seventy-five years later describes the voyage. There are no other records of Corte-Real's "discovery."

João Vaz's sons, Gaspar and Miguel, were also sailors and probably *did* sail to Newfoundland. But if so, they came after Columbus. Only their mysterious father may have beaten the great Columbus.

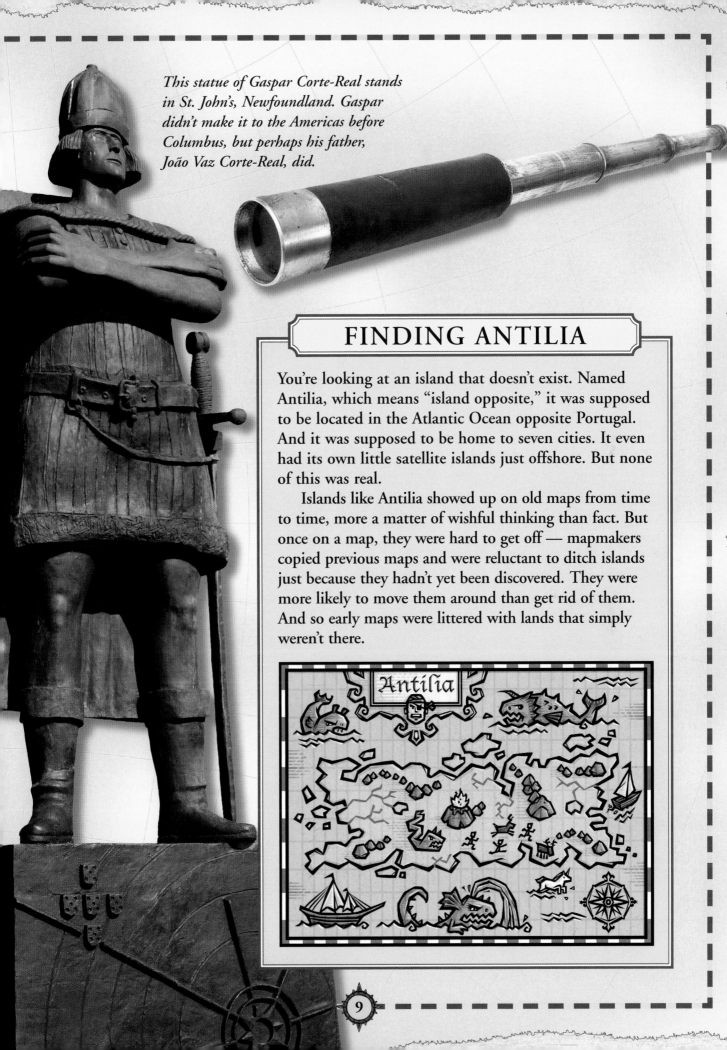

This statue of Gaspar Corte-Real stands in St. John's, Newfoundland. Gaspar didn't make it to the Americas before Columbus, but perhaps his father, João Vaz Corte-Real, did.

FINDING ANTILIA

You're looking at an island that doesn't exist. Named Antilia, which means "island opposite," it was supposed to be located in the Atlantic Ocean opposite Portugal. And it was supposed to be home to seven cities. It even had its own little satellite islands just offshore. But none of this was real.

Islands like Antilia showed up on old maps from time to time, more a matter of wishful thinking than fact. But once on a map, they were hard to get off — mapmakers copied previous maps and were reluctant to ditch islands just because they hadn't yet been discovered. They were more likely to move them around than get rid of them. And so early maps were littered with lands that simply weren't there.

SWIMMING DRAGONS

THEN THERE ARE THE CHINESE. IN THE early 1400s, "swimming dragons" set out from China to explore the world. The dragons — actually a fleet of ships — were enormous, many with decks bigger than a football field. Their masts, as many as nine per ship, pierced the sky like the spines on the back of a giant dragon. And painted on them were huge eyes — dragon eyes.

This replica of Admiral Zheng He's largest treasure boat is 1.2 m (4 ft.) long. The real thing would have been 134 m (440 ft.) long.

These ships were under the command of Admiral Zheng He (pronounced "jung huh"), and they gathered treasure from cities in Asia, India, Arabia and Africa. Then, in 1421, some of these ships, or perhaps smaller versions of them, sailed around the tip of Africa and north until they caught the prevailing winds that swept them to South America — seventy-two years before Columbus discovered America. Within two years, other Chinese ships had explored both coasts of North America.

Or, at least, that's what retired British Navy commander Gavin Menzies thinks. In the early 1990s, he began poring over old maps in search of clues that the Chinese had made

Columbus's largest ship, the Santa Maria (in gray), would have been dwarfed by a Chinese treasure ship.

it to the Americas long before Columbus. He even sailed some of the routes he believes the Chinese took. Unfortunately, the records of Admiral Zheng He's voyages were destroyed. Without more evidence, Menzies' theory is just that — a theory.

But Paul Chiasson, a Canadian architect, thinks he does have proof. While out hiking one day near his birthplace in Cape Breton, Nova Scotia, he came across an old stone road halfway up a wooded hillside. When he returned to his home in Toronto, Chiasson couldn't get this ghostly road out of his mind. But no matter how much he searched, he could find no record of when it was used or who built it.

He didn't give up. In May 2004, Chiasson followed the road again and came across walls and evidence of a huge settlement on the hillside. He found what looked to him to be the remains of a town, nearby farms and even a graveyard. His architectural training told him these ruins were not like others in the area, which had been left by the French. No, the ruins looked … Chinese. And Chiasson thinks that the island of Antilia (see "Finding Antilia" on page 9) that appeared on early maps wasn't just a figment of mapmakers' imaginations but was, in fact, Cape Breton — and that it was discovered by the Chinese.

Time, and archaeological study, will tell whether Paul Chiasson's ruins are Chinese. And evidence may surface that proves — or disproves — Gavin Menzies' theory that Admiral Zheng He's fleet reached the Americas long before Columbus.

But however this chapter turns out, the story doesn't end with the Chinese. Far from it …

IT'S IN THE BONES

Convincing evidence that the Chinese discovered America has yet to be found. But in 2006, some hard evidence turned up that pointed to an even earlier group of travelers to the Americas. Scientists unearthed some 600-year-old chicken bones in an ancient settlement in Chile. By analyzing the DNA of one of the bones, they could tell that it came from Polynesia. How did the bones get from Polynesia 3600 km (2200 mi.) across the Pacific Ocean to Chile? Someone must have brought the chickens by boat. Yes, the bones suggest that Polynesians had reached the Americas at least eighty-five years before Columbus. But were they the first?

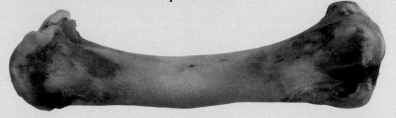

KNIGHTS AND NOBLES

A girl poses beside the image of the Westford knight, which has been outlined in chalk so that you can see it more clearly. Without the chalk, there are just a few scratches.

THE FARTHER BACK YOU GO, THE MURKIER things tend to get. Here are two very murky stories about the discovery of the Americas before Columbus, even before the somewhat murky Chinese tale.

Story No. 1: In 1558, Nicolo Zeno from Venice wrote a book about his ancestors and a journey they had taken. In the year 1400, Zeno claimed, his ancestors, two brothers, had sailed with one Prince Zichmni from an island near Scotland to Greenland. It was a long voyage for the time, and some thought Zeno had made the whole thing up.

Years passed. Then in 1786, a British scientist named J.R. Forster read the Zeno book and came up with the theory that Prince Zichmni was really a Scottish earl named Henry Sinclair. Others took up the story and added details. Sinclair, they said, hadn't stopped at Greenland but had sailed all the way to the Americas — more than ninety years before Columbus. The idea of a Scot discovering America took off. More details were added: Sinclair had landed in what is now Nova Scotia, then traveled south to Massachusetts and Rhode Island before returning to Scotland, where he was killed in a battle.

The proof? Supporters say that carvings in Henry Sinclair's Scottish home of Rosslyn are of plants that are found only in the Americas. So Sinclair must have been to the new world and brought back plants. Then there's an old Venetian cannon found in Nova Scotia in 1849 (could it have belonged to the Zenos?) and an old stone tower in Newport, Rhode Island (could it have been built by Sinclair?). And finally there is the Westford Knight.

In the small town of Westford, Massachusetts, there is a stone that some people think has been carved with the image of a knight to honor a man who traveled with Sinclair and died there. But there are many who doubt the story. Some towns-people think a group of boys carved the stone as a prank in the late 1800s. And some historians claim the marks on the stone aren't engravings at all, just scratches made when the stone was pushed along by a glacier long ago.

Did a Scot discover America more than ninety years before Columbus? What do you think?

Story No. 2: Around the year 1170, Prince Madoc of Wales wanted to flee the fighting that had broken out between his brothers and sailed off with a fleet of boats. He returned two years later, claiming he had found a wonderful new land. His stories so intrigued people that they wanted to join him. He set off again, this time with ten ships full of sightseers.

Those who believe the story think the Welsh ships landed in Mobile Bay in Alabama. They point to ruins in the area that look like Welsh forts, not forts made by the aboriginal people. They believe the Welsh fought with nearby aboriginal groups and were forced to move inland. There, they met a friendly people called the Mandan.

The proof? Take a look at the boats on this page. The one on the right is a Welsh boat called a coracle. The boats in the painting below look very similar to coracles. The painting depicts a Mandan village in the 1830s. Some people think the Mandan intermarried with the Welsh and learned their customs, including how to build coracles. A few early explorers even claimed they had met blond, fair-skinned Mandan, who looked … well, Welsh.

So … Welsh forts, Welsh

boats and Welsh-looking aboriginal people. Is it enough to convince you that the Welsh Prince Madoc discovered America in 1170, 322 years before Columbus?

NORSE FROM THE NORTH

TRAVELING BACK FARTHER NOW, WE MEET a much stronger contender.

Long ago, sagas (stories) were told about Vikings sailing from their home in Greenland to a new land called Vinland about the year 1000. Many people thought the sagas were just stories, but others began to wonder if they were records of an actual journey. If so, where exactly was this Vinland? It was a mystery that several people were trying to solve.

One of the "detectives" was a Norwegian historian named Helge Ingstad. He and his wife, archaeologist Anne Stine Ingstad, had studied Viking ruins in Greenland. They believed the sagas were true and had a hunch that Vinland was somewhere in Newfoundland.

In 1960, Helge traveled along the coast of Newfoundland, visiting isolated outports in search of evidence that Vikings had been there long ago. In the small community of L'Anse aux Meadows, he asked a local man if there were ruins nearby. The man replied, "Yes, follow me!" and led Helge to a meadow near a creek. Dotted around the meadow were some unimpressive forms that Ingstad described as "overgrown mounds."

The Viking settlement at L'Anse aux Meadows has been reconstructed to look the way it did when the Vikings lived there 1000 years ago. The buildings had wood frames, thick sod walls and heavy sod roofs. Judging by their size, the place was once home to about 100 people.

But later, when Anne Stine began carefully excavating the mounds, the results were amazing. (At an excavation, archaeologists dig down through the soil and carefully recover artifacts and other clues about the past. They record the location of everything they find.) As the sod was carefully peeled back and the soil cleared away, they found the remains of homes, workshops and even a furnace hut (a place where iron was smelted).

Over eleven summers of excavations, archaeologists uncovered many artifacts that were not from the area, such as a glass bead, part of a spindle used to spin wool, objects made of wood from Europe and many iron boat nails. The real showstopper was the ringed pin you see here. It was made of bronze (a material that was not produced in North America until much later), and it was identical to pins used by the Vikings as primitive safety pins.

The ringed pin was physical proof that the Vikings had been there. When it was uncovered, Anne Stine later recalled, "We practically exploded in our excitement."

Thanks to the excavation of L'Anse aux Meadows, we now know this much: Columbus did not discover America. The Vikings were there long before him and left solid evidence to prove it.

But this is still not the end of the story …

THE VIKINGS ARE COMING!

In the year 986, a Viking named Bjarni Herjólfsson was sailing to Greenland when he hit bad weather. He was blown off course and saw a lush new land, probably North America. Another Viking, Leif Erikson, heard Bjarni's story and decided to try to find this new land for himself.

He sailed from Greenland with a ship of about thirty-five people. On the coast of Newfoundland he established a camp at L'Anse aux Meadows and explored the area, gathering timber and other valuable resources. After he returned to Greenland, he let other family members use his settlement. In all, L'Anse aux Meadows was probably occupied for about fifteen years.

TO AMERICA IN A LEATHER BOAT

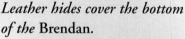

Leather hides cover the bottom of the Brendan.

ENTER THE IRISH. MORE THAN 400 YEARS before the Vikings, Saint Brendan and seventeen monks are said to have left Ireland in a leather boat and sailed to a new land. Some people think the new land was North America, making Saint Brendan the first to get there. Others think the Brendan story, written down hundreds of years after his death, is just a folktale. After all, how could a small, primitive boat make it across the treacherous North Atlantic?

In 1976, Tim Severin, a British historian and adventurer, decided to find out. He gathered together boat builders, leather tanners and rope makers to create a replica of Saint Brendan's leather boat. Forty-nine ox hides were tanned in an oak-bark mixture and dipped into a vat of grease from sheep's wool to waterproof them. Then the hides were draped over the wooden frame of the boat and sewn together by hand with some 30 000 painstaking and painful stitches. Another coat of wool grease and the *Brendan*, as she was named, was ready to go.

On launch day, the *Brendan* proved herself. She was tricky to sail at first and a bit of water seeped in, but soon the crew got used to her and the leaking stopped. The plan was to hop from island to island all the way from Ireland to Iceland. That way the crew could go ashore for fresh supplies of food and water and, if necessary, repair the boat. Past Iceland, they would sweep along Greenland and Labrador to Newfoundland, where they thought Saint Brendan may have landed long ago.

Two days out of their Irish harbor, a rainstorm hit the leather boat, and the wild weather continued for much of the trip. They almost missed one group of islands when they were blown off course by heavy winds. There were some calm days, when the whales would come to inspect them, fascinated by the whalelike leather hull of the *Brendan*. At one point more than 100 pilot whales swam under the ship, taking turns to surface and have a closer look. Mostly, though, it was cold and stormy. By the time they reached Iceland, winter was approaching. They would have to wait until the next spring to attempt the rest of the voyage.

Spring 1977 in the North Atlantic brought one gale after another. Slicing rain, stomach-churning waves and cold that could numb fingers and faces in minutes made life onboard miserable — and wet. Water got into the sleeping bags, into the food, into everything.

And then things got worse. One night, crinkling sounds were heard by those sleeping below deck. The sleepy, soggy crew clambered up and could hardly believe their eyes. They were sailing through a soup of ice, from small chunks to icebergs taller than a house. And the only thing that stood between them and the icy water was a layer of leather not much thicker than a banana peel.

Twenty-four hours of steering through the ice left everyone exhausted. Then, two huge ice floes caught the *Brendan* between them and squeezed. The *Brendan*'s leather skin was punctured, and only nonstop pumping kept her afloat. When day broke, a bit of luck. They found the hole and managed to sew on a patch. A week later, on June 26, 1977, the *Brendan* landed in Newfoundland.

The modern-day *Brendan* proved that Saint Brendan could have discovered North America almost 1000 years before Columbus. But "could have" and "did" are not the same thing. Until evidence of long-ago Irish is found in North America, the story of the sailing monk remains just a story.

A water pipit lands on Tim Severin. Birds often hitchhiked on the Brendan.

The Brendan *under sail.*

BEFORE THE EUROPEANS

George McJunkin, the cowboy who found the first clue.

NOTICE ANYTHING ODD ABOUT THE explorers you've read about so far? Although they were supposed to be the discoverers of the Americas, many of them reported meeting people who were already here. Yes, long before the Europeans (or maybe the Chinese or Polynesians) set foot in the Americas, the land was inhabited by the aboriginal people. Did *they* actually discover the Americas? And if so, when did they do it?

For a long time, people thought that the ancestors of modern Native Americans first appeared here about 5000 years ago. But then a Black cowboy named George McJunkin made a discovery that turned back the clock.

McJunkin managed a ranch near Folsom, New Mexico. One scorching hot August day in 1908, he rode into Wild Horse Arroyo, a dried-out stream bed. Rains had caused flooding that ripped away part of the arroyo, exposing some bison bones and a spear point.

McJunkin was intrigued. The bones were bigger than any bison bones he had ever seen. They, and the spear point, looked old — very old.

For many years, no one seemed much interested in McJunkin's find. He died before the bones (and other, later discoveries of bones and spear points) came to the attention of scientists. When scientists finally investigated, they were shocked.

The bones were of a long-extinct species of bison that roamed the earth at the end of the last ice age, some 10 000 years ago. And the spear points found among them suggested that people wielding spears were there during the ice age, too.

Ten thousand years ago! Who were these ancient people?

The bones you see here belonged to an ice-age bison that died when a spear pierced its side. The spear point is circled in red. The wooden shaft of the spear disintegrated over time.

FASTEN YOUR SEATBELT: YOU ARE ENTERING PREHISTORY ...

There are no written accounts or histories of the earliest North Americans. This time period was prehistory. So how do we know about them? Archaeologists look for artifacts (physical remains such as bones, tools and baskets) the ancients left behind. These artifacts can tell a lot about who the people were and when they lived.

Many Native Americans believe that their legends and stories, rather than artifacts, are evidence of their long-ago ancestors. These legends and stories say that the Native people have always been here — that they are definitely the first people.

CLOVIS FIRST?

McJUNKIN'S ICE-AGE BONES AND THE spear points found near Folsom, New Mexico, may have set the clock for the discovery of the Americas at an amazing 10 000 years ago. But the clock was soon to be turned back even farther, this time by a teenager named Ridge Whiteman.

Ridge Whiteman

Ridge's mother was a collector of arrowheads, and Ridge himself was interested in long-ago aboriginal life. In 1929, at age 19, he spotted a sharp-edged stone glinting in the dry soil of Blackwater Draw near Clovis, New Mexico. The stone blade was no arrowhead. It was almost as big as the palm of his hand and shaped like a long leaf. It also had a flute (groove) at its base.

Ridge sent the blade and a mammoth tooth he had found to an amateur archaeologist named Edgar Billings Howard. Howard started a careful excavation at Blackwater Draw in 1933.

At first, Howard found Folsom-style spear points. Then, digging deeper, he discovered stone blades like the one Ridge Whiteman had sent him.

It was a major find. The deeper an artifact is located, the older it is. (Think of garbage in a can; the stuff lower down went in earlier. It's older than the stuff higher up.) Finding a new style of spear point in a layer of soil underneath the Folsom points indicated that a different and earlier people had been in the area. And mammoth bones nearby suggested they were mammoth hunters.

These early people were named Clovis people after the nearby town. Gradually, more and more Clovis spear points were found over large parts of North America. Radiocarbon dating (see "How old is old?") showed that the Clovis spear points had been made in North America about 11 500 years ago. This exciting news raised the old questions: Where had these people come from? And were *they* the first?

HOW OLD IS OLD?

The rule "the deeper, the older" is a useful one. It can tell you if one spear point is older than another by its position in the soil (the deeper one is older). But what if you want to know how many years old the points are? Radiocarbon dating to the rescue!

Everything that lives (plant or animal) contains carbon 14, a radioactive form of carbon that decays steadily over time. The amount of carbon 14 left in, say, a bone or piece of wood tells you how old it is.

But what if you found a stone spear point and wanted to know how old *it* was? Stone doesn't contain carbon, so radiocarbon dating won't work. Instead, scientists look for bones or wood or other organic things at the same depth as the spear point. By carbon dating these objects, they can also date the spear point.

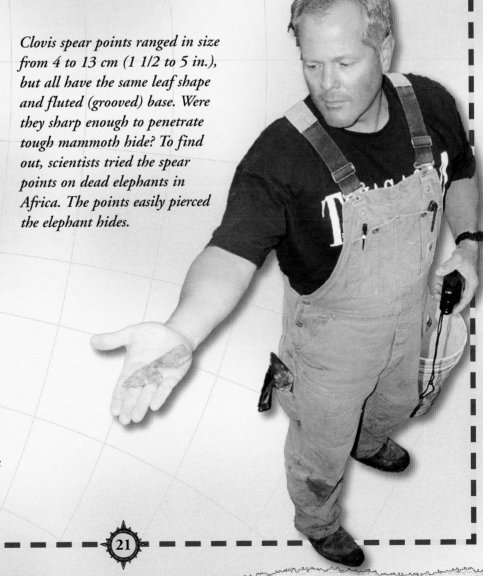

Clovis spear points ranged in size from 4 to 13 cm (1 1/2 to 5 in.), but all have the same leaf shape and fluted (grooved) base. Were they sharp enough to penetrate tough mammoth hide? To find out, scientists tried the spear points on dead elephants in Africa. The points easily pierced the elephant hides.

GETTING HERE

IMAGINE STEPPING BACK INTO SIBERIA 11 500 years ago. The climate is colder than today's, and huge glaciers cover much of the land. Hope you wore a coat, because you've landed in an ice age.

The cold is the bad news — it's hard to find food with all the ice and snow. But there is some good news. Enormous glaciers have locked up so much of the world's water into ice that the sea level has dropped. A huge patch of land is now exposed, connecting Siberia and Alaska like a bridge. Maybe hunters wandered across this land bridge in search of game.

Until recently, scientists had a theory about the Clovis people that went like this: They traveled across the Bering land bridge (named for the Bering Sea, which now covers it) from Siberia into Alaska. From there, they moved south through a narrow, ice-free corridor between two huge Canadian ice sheets. Over the next 500 years or so, the Clovis people and their descendants moved swiftly into North America, rapidly fanning out across the whole continent and into South America. Along the way, they hunted big animals, such as mammoths. In fact, they were so fast and ferocious that they hunted the big animals to extinction.

The Bering land "bridge" was actually a huge area of land that once connected Siberia and Alaska. It is shown in brown here.

Ice sheets like these were as thick as 2.4 km (1 1/2 mi.) at certain times and places during the last ice age.

But that picture of the Clovis people began to change as more and more evidence was found. It now appears that they mostly ate berries and other plants gathered from the wild, as well as small animals such as turtles, alligators and foxes. Big animals would have been a minor part of their diet. And they didn't travel fast. Instead, they lived in settled groups at certain places over long periods of time.

And here was the big news: the Clovis people weren't the first to discover the Americas. Because before the Clovis people spread through North America, a different people were already living in South America ...

YOU ARE WHAT YOU LEAVE BEHIND

Picture the world 10 000 years in the future. What if only our pens survived? Would future scientists think we were all authors?

In the case of ancient people, it's mostly their stone tools and weapons that survived. But these artifacts make up only about 5 percent of the things a group of people used. The rest of their things (clothing, woven baskets, nets, tents, etc.) are made from plants or animal parts and usually disintegrate over the years.

Finding only stone artifacts can mislead scientists. The abundance of Clovis spear points, for example, led scientists to believe that the people who made them were big game hunters and big mammoth eaters, until new evidence painted a different picture.

Did Clovis people kill mammoths for food? The cut marks on these mammoth bones and the number of bones found near spear points suggest they did. But now we know they ate mostly plants and small animals.

MONTE VERDE

Monte Verde

IN 1977, A YOUNG ARCHAEOLOGIST NAMED Tom Dillehay came across a time capsule from the last ice age — a perfectly preserved settlement in southern Chile.

Normally, time takes its toll on things buried in the ground. But Monte Verde, as the site was called, had escaped this fate. Not long after people had lived there, a creek had risen and made the land marshy. Then a layer of peat (dense plant material) had covered it, so that air had not been able to get to the artifacts and cause decay.

Carefully digging down through time, Dillehay and his team uncovered stone tools, which was to be expected. But they also found evidence of cooking fires and skin tents and the food the people ate, including nuts, berries, mushrooms, wild potatoes, small animals and mastodons (huge elephantlike ice-age animals). There was even a preserved chunk of mastodon meat.

About 12 500 years ago, a teenager left this footprint in some clay that lined a fire pit at Monte Verde. It was the only trace of the people themselves. No human bones have been found.

Who were these South Americans and where were they from? They couldn't have been Siberians who came over the Bering land bridge because the ice-free corridor that allowed people into North America hadn't existed then. So how had the people got here? Maybe finding out how they came would tell us where they came from — and whether they discovered the Americas.

The site had been home to twenty to thirty people. Judging by the artifacts, they had lived in large, hide-covered, tentlike structures with separate rooms. Outside, there had been another structure, where butchering and tool making took place, and even a "medical clinic," where remains of medicinal plants were found. Some of these plants were from nearby and are still used by the local people today to cure illnesses, but others were from far away. This suggests that the original inhabitants may have traded with other groups to get what they needed.

But the big surprise came with the radiocarbon dating. The samples that were tested were about 12 500 years old — 1000 years older than the Clovis people in North America.

IF THIS STICK COULD SPEAK

This stick, found at Monte Verde, Chile, is about 12 500 years old. If you came across it, what would you say it was? A branch or tree root?

To archaeologists, the piece of reed carefully knotted around it suggested it was a tent peg. The use of reeds to tie things also told them that people had been in Monte Verde long enough to become familiar with local plants. Amazing the tale a stick can tell.

SEAFARERS

MONTE VERDE AND OTHER SOUTH American sites showed that there had been people in the Americas before the Clovis people. And as archaeologists began digging deeper at several sites in North America, they, too, found evidence of an earlier people. How did these pre-Clovis people get to the Americas before the ice-free corridor opened up about 12 000 years ago?

It was time for archaeologists to ask "What if?" What if these people had traveled by boat down the west coast of North America? That way, they could have arrived in the Americas before the ice-free corridor opened. But a coastal route was only possible if early people could have found food along the way, and that was a big "if."

Traveling along the coast by boat, this is what you might have seen — a wall of ice at the edge of ice sheets that covered most of the land.

The huge ice sheets that covered Canada and the northern United States extended to the edges of the land, as in the picture you see here. So there was nowhere for plants or land animals to live (and therefore no food for seafaring hunters). It was time for another "What if?" What if there were small ice-free zones along the coast where hunters of marine mammals, such as seals, could land their boats and camp?

Finding evidence of such zones was going to be difficult — the ancient coastline was mostly underwater, submerged as the ice sheets melted. But give archaeologists a challenge and they will rise to it — or in this case, sink to it. Using sonar (underwater radar) to map the ancient sea floor and taking samples in places that might have been ancient campsites, they began looking for evidence of ice-free zones.

They found it. Pollen from plants suggested there were zones that could have been home to bears and other animals that might have served as food for seafarers. Later, submerged forests, rivers and ancient lakes were discovered. Then a stone tool was retrieved from a place on the sea floor that had been

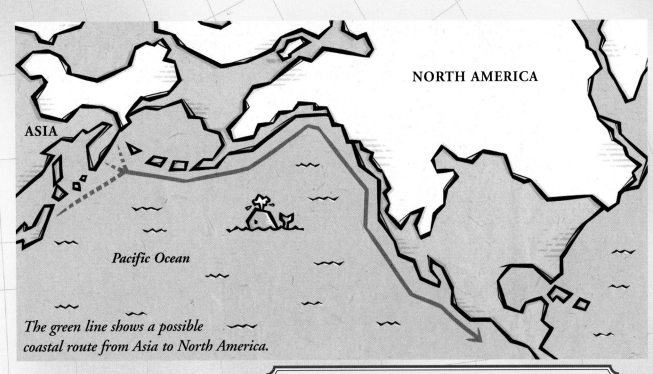

ASIA

NORTH AMERICA

Pacific Ocean

The green line shows a possible coastal route from Asia to North America.

exposed land 10 000 years ago. Hunters had been there!

Ice-free zones were also found on the edges of some islands, such as Haida Gwaii. Maybe people in small hide boats hopscotched southward from one ice-free zone to another, hunting and gathering as they went. Some may have stopped at places along the U.S. coast and moved inland, accounting for the sites there. Others might have continued down to South America. And it could have happened long before the ice-free corridor opened.

There were still a lot of "what ifs" and "maybes" rather than hard evidence, but the idea of a coastal migration was intriguing, especially when another piece of the puzzle fell into place with the discovery of some very old bones …

THE KELP HIGHWAY

Kelp is a seaweed that provides a habitat for birds, shellfish and sea mammals. Recently, a team of scientists has observed that there is an almost unbroken band of kelp stretching all along the shore of the North Pacific as far as Asia. This "kelp highway" might have been a useful route for ancient seafarers, providing them with food. And the kelp had another bonus for people in small boats. It reduces wave action, giving boaters a smoother and safer ride.

SKULL DIGGERY

HE WAS MIDDLE-AGED, ABOUT 1.75 M (5 ft. 9 in.) tall, and he was just a pile of bones when two university students found him in the mud along the Columbia River near Kennewick, Washington, in 1996. They called in the police, who treated the case like a homicide.

But if it was a homicide, it was one that had happened long, long ago. A spear point embedded in the hip alerted investigators to that, and the bones were sent for radiocarbon dating. The startling news? Kennewick Man, as he came to be called, was 9000 years old, making his remains among the oldest ever found in the Americas.

Enter the scientists and five local Indian tribes. The scientists wanted to study the bones. The Indians wanted them properly buried. The scientists went to court.

Only a few ancient skeletons have been found, and Kennewick Man is one of the most complete.

The case dragged on for nine years before the courts decided to release the bones to the scientists for study.

The bones revealed a lot. Kennewick Man had had a hard life. In addition to the spear in his hip, he had had arthritis in one elbow, a broken rib resulting from a blow to the chest and a skull fracture that suggested someone had hit him with a club. None of those injuries killed him, and the cause of death is not known.

But the position his body was found in — arms at his sides, palms down — suggests that he may have been deliberately buried. Someone must have cared about him.

One of the biggest discoveries was that Kennewick Man's skull was unlike Native American skulls. It was more like the skull of someone from the east coast of Asia. For some time, archaeologists had been wondering if people could have come all the way from

Asia to North America by boat. The kelp highway (see "The kelp highway" on page 27) did extend to Asia, making long-distance travel from there possible.

The skull of Kennewick Man seemed to say yes. Were the discoverers of the Americas ancient people from the east coast of Asia?

Fascinating. But hang on. This is still not the end of the story …

TALKING SKULLS

Your skull has certain features that connect you to your long-ago ancestors. Scientists use skull morphology (structure and shape) to try to connect old skulls to their ancestors. They take more than sixty measurements of such things as skull width and eye-socket size and then compare them with a worldwide data bank of skull measurements. When they find a match, they know they have connected a skull to its ancestral group.

Using skull morphology, scientists theorize that Kennewick Man may have been related to people from the east coast of Asia or possibly to the ancestors of the Ainu, the aboriginal people who still live in northern Japan. Other skulls found in North and South America show connections to other places in Asia, and to other places altogether.

Unfortunately, none of the skulls found so far can tell us where the first people came from — they are simply not old enough.

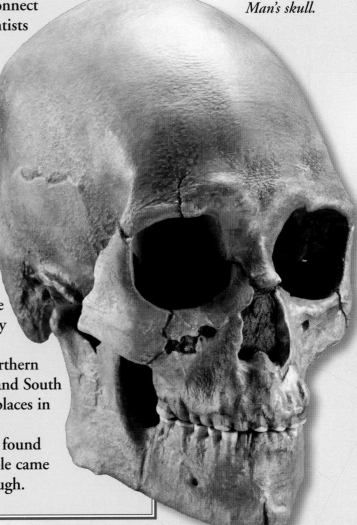

This is Kennewick Man's skull.

OR MAYBE THEY WERE EUROPEANS AFTER ALL

WHAT IF THE DISCOVERERS OF THE Americas weren't from Siberia or Asia at all? What if they turned out to be Europeans — not Columbus, the Vikings, the Irish or the Welsh but their much, much earlier ancestors?

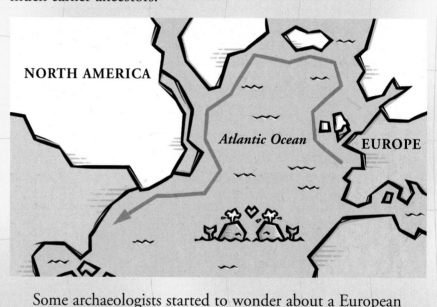

NORTH AMERICA

Atlantic Ocean

EUROPE

People from Europe may have traveled across the Atlantic in boats like this umiak, once used by the Inuit of Canada's Arctic. The Inuit hunted from these boats and then pulled them up onto the ice at night, overturned them and used them as shelters. Maybe the long-ago Solutreans did, too.

Some archaeologists started to wonder about a European connection after they noticed that spear points made by the ancient Solutrean people of Spain and France were very similar to the points of the Clovis people in North America. Both spear points were long, flat and leaf-shaped. More amazingly, both were made using the same method — called the overshot technique. A piece of bone or wood was pressed against a piece of stone, causing a shard to split off across the whole

This ordinary-looking sand dune at Cactus Hill produced evidence of a possible connection with ancient Europeans.

surface of the stone. The maker used this technique over and over to make the spear point very thin, so that it would penetrate better.

The overshot technique is difficult and unusual — so unusual that it was possible that there was a connection between the two peoples. Had the Solutreans traveled across the Atlantic Ocean to the Americas, settled there and passed the technique down to their descendants, the Clovis people? Could the Solutreans have been the first people to discover the Americas?

Wait one minute, said many archaeologists. The distance across the Atlantic is some 4800 km (3000 mi.), and much of the North Atlantic would have been covered by a huge ice sheet back then. No primitive people could have survived such a daunting trip. No problem, said other archaeologists. The Inuit of the Canadian north had traveled long distances in hide boats for thousands of years, hauling out

onto the ice to rest and hunt for food. If they traveled like the Inuit, ancient Europeans could have made it to the Americas in as little as three weeks.

But there was also a timing problem, said the doubters. The Solutreans had lived about 19 000 years ago, 6000 or so years before the Clovis

people. That's a big gap. But then, digs at a sand dune in Virginia called Cactus Hill turned up some spear points that looked a bit like Clovis points, only much older. In fact, the dates of these points meant there had been people at Cactus Hill at least 19 000 years ago.

So did Europeans cross the Atlantic and discover the Americas 19 000 or so years ago? Scientists are still debating the question. Some recent genetic studies (see "Tracking genes") offer tantalizing new clues.

TRACKING GENES

You inherit your genes from your parents, and they inherited genes from their parents, and so on back through time. Genes act like a chain to the past, and scientists can follow the links.

Recently, scientists have been tracking back the genes of Native Americans to see if they are linked to peoples elsewhere in the world. So far, research suggests a strong connection with the aboriginal people of Asia. No surprise there. But some Native Americans, such as the Ojibwa of the Great Lakes, also have a genetic link to peoples from Europe.

By tracing back the DNA (the carrier of genetic information in cells) of modern-day Native Americans, scientists have learned something else, too. They think there may have been as few as eighty people in the very first group to come to the Americas.

WERE THERE OTHERS?

ANCIENT ASIANS? LONG-AGO EUROPEANS?
As the field gets jam-packed with contenders, you have to ask, was there anybody else who had a claim to discovering the Americas?

As a matter of fact, yes. In Los Toldos Cave, near the tip of South America, Augusto Cardich, an Argentine archaeologist, dug up a new possibility. Stone scrapers and paintings on the cave walls suggested to Dr. Cardich a link with the ancient people of … Australia!

This is Los Toldos Cave, which was occupied by humans 14 000 years ago.

TALKING WITH THE DEAD

By tracing back the languages of the living, we can "talk" to the dead — or at least find out who they were and where they came from. That's what linguists (people who study languages) like Johanna Nichols believe. They analyze patterns in languages to find out when one language split off from another, and use these splits to track people back in time.

What do the languages of today's Native Americans tell us about the dead? Nichols theorizes that the 143 families of languages spoken by Native Americans resulted from groups coming along the North Pacific coast at different times from places such as Siberia, Southeast Asia and, yes, even Australia. Other linguists disagree. They say that almost all Native American languages evolved from a single ancient language.

The paintings were especially intriguing. Some were stencils of hands. Others were made of dots of paint in patterns of circles or spirals. To Dr. Cardich, they looked strikingly similar to Australian cave paintings. He also thought the scrapers were like ancient Australian tools.

People long ago put their hands on a wall in Los Toldos Cave and blew pigment around them to make these handprints, leaving their personal marks for thousands of years.

This idea was definitely a long shot. Could people from as far away as Australia have made it all the way to South America? The distance was huge, far greater than the distance from Europe to the Americas. And the seas from Australia to South America are among the roughest in the world. Even today's high-tech boats can get into trouble there.

Still, Dr. Cardich isn't willing to give up on the idea. The Australians and South Pacific islanders had been building and sailing boats for thousands of years, he says. It's possible that these experienced boaters could have hopped from island to island and then been blown by the prevailing winds to America.

Possible, but not likely. What's missing is physical evidence that links sites in the Americas with Australia. But in archaeology, where everything is hidden underground — or underwater — just because something hasn't been found yet doesn't mean it isn't there.

LONG AGO AND FAR OUT

 IN 2005, THREE SCIENTISTS WHO WERE studying the rocks of Toluquilla Quarry near Mexico City found footprints — 269 in all — preserved in rock. Some appeared to be made by animals, but more than half looked like human footprints, including some small ones made by children.

Radiocarbon dating of lake silt from the same level dated the footprints at 40 000 years. The news was sensational. The footprints were a whopping 20 000 years older than any other accepted evidence of people in the Americas. Newspapers jumped to cover the story, and so did the other media. But then more scientists got involved. They were not convinced. Either the dating must be wrong or these were not footprints.

How did these footprints get into the rock? The scientists who found them believe a nearby volcano blew its top 40 000 years ago, scattering ash onto the shore of a lake. People walked through the ash, which was gradually turned into mud, then rock, preserving their footprints. But other scientists are not so sure that the prints are footprints. What do you think? The pen shows the size of the marks.

Some skeptical scientists took new samples. This time they used argon dating and paleomagnetic analysis, two other methods that are good for dating very old things.

The news was even more stunning. The rock in which the footprints were found now dated at more than a million years. Could people have discovered the Americas that long ago?

No way, say most scientists. That's just too old. It goes against all ideas of how the earliest humans populated the Earth. These couldn't be footprints, just gouges in the rock, possibly caused by erosion or the activities of modern quarry workers. But the three scientists who found the marks in the rock are not giving up. They say the latest testing was flawed. Until more tests are done, no one knows for sure.

And no one may ever know for sure. The long-ago past holds tightly onto its secrets, and the way we view the clues we find may say as much about us as it does about the past.

LEAKEY'S LUCK RUNS OUT

Louis Leakey was one lucky (and famous) archaeologist. With the help of his wife, Mary, he had found key evidence in Africa about the origins of early humans. But Louis Leakey's luck ran out in the Mojave Desert of the United States in 1963.

He had come to the desert to look at a site called Calico Hills. There, in a trench, he spotted what looked to be very old stone tools in a layer that was more than 50 000 years old. A find that old would overturn all ideas about when people first came to the Americas. Leakey was elated. But wait. Were the tools really tools, or were they just rocks that had had edges chipped off in a mini-avalanche? In the opinion of other archaeologists, the rocks were just rocks. The moral: even the famous can be misled by nature's tricks.

If you found *this* stone, would you think it was chipped by humans or that nature did the chipping? Turn to page 38 to find out.

WHO DUNNIT AND WHEN DID IT ALL HAPPEN?

THE AMERICAS WERE ONE OF THE LAST areas on Earth to be inhabited. *Homo sapiens* (our long-ago ancestors) began life in Africa about 150 000 years ago and had spread north into Europe, east into Asia and south into Australia by about 40 000 years ago. All this time, there were probably no people in the Americas.

So who was first to discover the Americas?

It definitely wasn't Christopher Columbus. Nor was it any of the other Europeans or the Chinese explorers. The aboriginal people were here long before any of them. Some of their ancestors, probably from Asia or Europe, may well have been the discoverers of the Americas. But the identity of the very first person — the man or woman who truly discovered the Americas — remains, and will always remain, one of the world's great mysteries.

TIMELINE

WHEN DID IT ALL HAPPEN? THIS TIMELINE shows some of the main contenders and the approximate dates they came to the Americas. As you can see, Columbus wasn't the first — he was actually the last in a long line of possible discoverers.

Today

2000 BP

4000 BP

6000 BP

8000 BP

10 000 BP

12 000 BP

14 000 BP

16 000 BP

18 000 BP

20 000 BP

22 000 BP

24 000 BP

26 000 BP

28 000 BP

30 000 BP

32 000 BP

34 000 BP

36 000 BP

38 000 BP

40 000 BP

Christopher Columbus (1492 AD), page 6

João Vaz Corte-Real (1472 AD), page 8

Admiral Zheng He's fleet (1421 AD), page 10

Henry Sinclair (1400 AD), page 12

Prince Madoc (1170 AD), page 13

The Norse (1000 AD), page 14

Saint Brendan (560 AD), page 16

Kennewick Man (9000 BP), page 28

The Clovis people (11 500 BP), page 20

The people of Monte Verde and other parts of South America (12 500–14 000 BP), pages 24 and 32

The Solutreans from Europe (19 000 BP), page 30

BP means Before Present

The people of Toluquilla Quarry, Mexico (40 000 BP), page 34

Who chipped this stone?

Sometimes it's hard to tell whether a human hand or nature has caused the chips and flakes on a rock. So archaeologists have a rule. A tool made by humans would show two or more of the following:

1. Three or more of the flakes are chipped off.
2. The places where the flakes are removed are weathered at the same rate, suggesting that the flakes were chipped off about the same time, not thousands of years apart.
3. There is a pattern to the way the flakes are chipped off. Humans usually work in a way that leaves a pattern.

This stone on the left, above, has only one flake (1). Because of this, it's not possible to check for uniform weathering (2). And it shows no even and regular pattern

of chipping (3). Archaeologists looking at this stone would probably conclude it was chipped by nature.

By contrast, this rock (above) *is* a tool. Notice the multiple chips, uniform weathering and regular chipping.

WHO NAMED AMERICA?

The name America first appeared on a map in 1507, but just how it got its name is in dispute. It may have been named after a gold-rich part of South America called Amerrique, which Columbus had heard of. Or after a customs official in Bristol, England, named Richard Ameryk, who knew the explorer John Cabot. Or it could come from a Viking term — Ommerike, meaning "farthest outland." But the most likely source of the name was Amerigo Vespucci. He explored the Americas just a few years after Columbus and was first to realize it was not just part of Asia but a brand-new land.

GLOSSARY

archaeological sites: any place where past people left remains of their activities.

artifacts: objects made and used by people. Artifacts found at archaeological sites are evidence of past peoples. Most of these artifacts, such as stone tools, weapons, pottery and bones, are composed of harder materials rather than softer, organic materials such as fabrics, leather, wood and plants, which wear away and disappear over time.

Bering land bridge: a natural land connection between Siberia and Alaska across what is now the Bering Strait. It appeared as more land was exposed when the sea levels dropped during the last ice age.

dating: applying technical tests to determine the age of an artifact. Radiocarbon dating is one common method, but there are other methods as well. Dating tells scientists when people who left the artifact lived.

DNA: short for deoxyribonucleic acid, this is the material inside the cells of our bodies that carries genetic information and passes it from one generation to the next.

excavations: parts of archaeological sites that are carefully dug up by scientists to look for artifacts and other evidence of people from the past.

genes: pieces of DNA by which traits, such as hair and eye color, are inherited.

ice-free corridor: a route between huge ice sheets in Western Canada, which opened at the end of the ice age, allowing people to move from Alaska into the lower United States. It was once thought to be the only entryway for the first people into North America, but now there are theories of other routes.

prehistory: a time before recorded history. Since there are no written records, we learn about how people lived in this time from artifacts and other evidence left behind.

radiocarbon dating: a way of dating artifacts by measuring the amount of carbon 14 contained in them or in nearby organic materials.

spear points: the pointed stone or bone ends attached to spear shafts. Because the shafts were made of wood, they disintegrate, leaving only the points.

INDEX